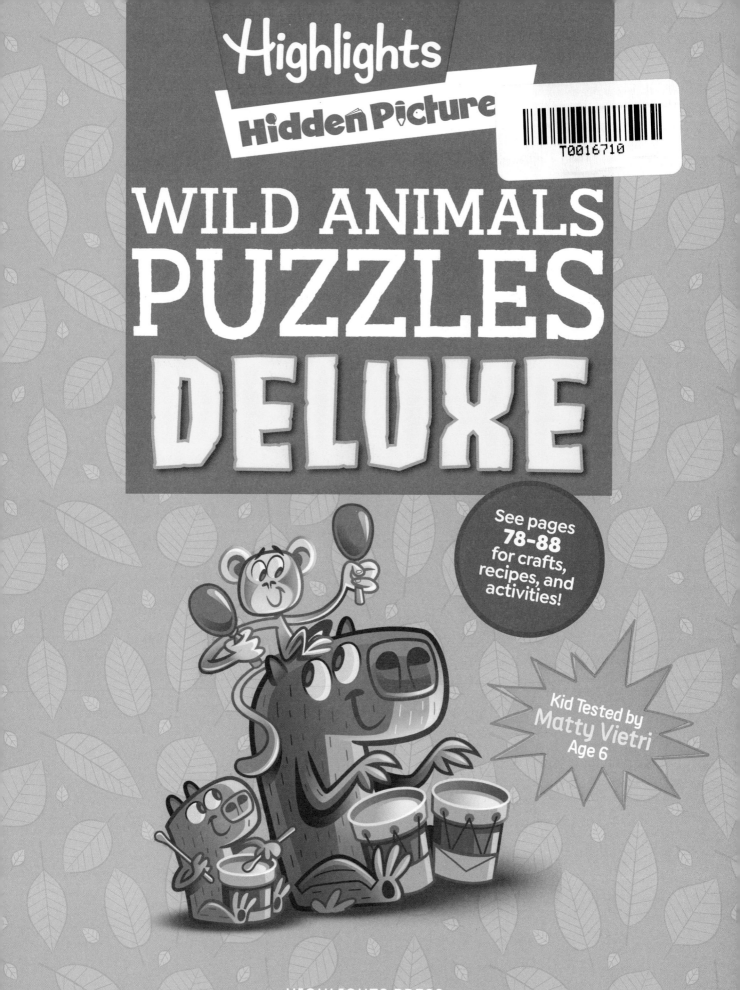

Highlights
Hidden Picture

WILD ANIMALS PUZZLES DELUXE

See pages
78–88
for crafts,
recipes, and
activities!

Kid Tested by
Matty Vietri
Age 6

HIGHLIGHTS PRESS
Honesdale, Pennsylvania

Pollinators in Training

tennis racket

needle

umbrella

football

kite

tweezers

baseball

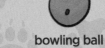
raindrop

glove

bowling ball

bow tie

belt

frying pan

bell

shovel

teacup

paid of pants

feather duster

heart

slice of pie

canoe

baseball cap

ruler

ring

golf tee

Art by Paula Becker

3

Desert Days

The sun is shining! See if you can find the hidden objects around these traveling camels.

knitted hat

ice-cream cone

pencil

mushroom

crown

kite

bow

slice of bacon

baseball bat

lightning bolt

vase

party hat

slice of pizza

leaf

paintbrush

baseball

window

cookie

cloud

flashlight

mug

shark

wave

log

sailboat

open book

sock

mitten

Art by Joey Ellis

Just Sayin'

Give this hippo something to say. Then find the hidden crescent moon, heart, slice of pie, sock, and wishbone.

Art by Felipe Galindo Gómez

How does a hippo cheer?

"Hip-hippo-ray!"

What kind of key opens a banana?

A monkey

5

Each of these small scenes contains **6** hidden objects from the list below. Some objects are hidden in more than one scene. Can you find the **6** hidden objects in each scene?

Hidden Object List

The numbers tell you how many times each object is hidden.

artist's brush (2)

banana (3)

boomerang (2)

broccoli (3)

comb (3)

crown (4)

hockey stick (2)

lightning bolt (2)

lollipop (3)

mitten (5)

paper clip (3)

pencil (4)

BONUS
Two scenes contain the exact same set of hidden objects. Can you find that matching pair?

Art by Brian Michael Weaver

Foxes in the Forest

See if you can find the hidden objects while these foxes play hide-and-seek.

baseball bat

car

ladder

closed umbrella

teapot

broccoli

saw

glove

boot

fried egg

pencil

artist's brush

comb

fish

key

football

Art by Lee Cosgrove

8

Hide It!

sock

dustpan

party hat

eyeglasses

clock

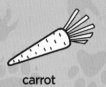
carrot

fork

glove

drinking
straw

pepper

pencil

comb

Art by Iryna Bodnaruk

11

Making Maple Syrup

Can you find at least 17 differences between these two pictures?

What do cowboys put on their pancakes?

Maple stirrup

What often falls but never gets hurt?

Snow

Art by Mike Brownlow

13

Plains Bike Race

pencil

baseball bat

scissors

toaster

ice-cream cone

 pan

fishing pole

envelope

button

fish

14

And they're off! Can you find all the hidden objects?

slice of pizza

wedge of cheese

ruler

sailboat

butterfly

banana

comb

boomerang

magnifying glass

glove

Frolicking Frogs

While the frogs splash around, can you find all the hidden objects?

trowel

strawberry

star

artist's brush

lollipop

efl's hat

fork

banana

slice of pizza

chicken

paper clip

taco

wishbone

wedge of lemon

shell

chili pepper

firefighter's helmet

pea pod

Art by Gary Mohrman

Can you find at least 18 differences between these two pictures?

Art by Joey Ellis

Take Two

Each of these scenes contains 12 hidden objects, which are listed below. Find each object in one of the scenes, then cross it off the list.

banana	fishhook	ice-cream cone	ruler
candle	fried egg	paper clip	slice of lime
cane	glove	paper airplane	slice of pie
carrot	golf club	pear	strawberry
crown	heart	pencil	tent
envelope	horseshoe	ring	toothbrush

Summer Fun

See if you can find the hidden objects while these sloths play outside.

soap

surfboard

six

seahorse

saw

sailboat

sandwich

seal

sock

seed

Glacial Navigation

Can you help this penguin slip and slide down a path to the water? Be careful not to crash into any other penguins.

START

FINISH

Art by Dan McGeehan

Art by Gareth Lucas

Tic Tac Row

What do the birds in each row (horizontally, vertically, and diagonally) have in common?

Art by Wayno

What is a bird's favorite cookie?

Chocolate chirp

Which birds like to stick together?

Vel-crows

24

Fun Down Under

Which things in this picture are silly? It's up to you!

Snail Mail

tweezers

sailboat

leash

slice of bread

chain

wedge of cheese

peach

iron

needle

peapod

shield

Art by Laura Watson

bowl

arrow

pie

bee

Moseying Moles

It's time for spelunking.
Can you find all the hidden objects?

teacup

artist's brush

ice-cream cone

ruler

ice-cream bar

slice of pizza

pencil

crescent moon

glove

button

frying pan

comb

adhesive bandage

sock

potato

snake

envelope

yo-yo

carrot

tack

bowling pin

Art by Brian Michael Weaver

Flamingo Dance

There are eight words (not pictures!) hidden in this scene. Can you find BEACH, BIRD, DANCE, PINK, SAND, SUN, TUTU, and TWIRL?

Art by Pat Lewis

Words and Objects

Art by Brian White

What did the beaver
say to the tree?

What's a beaver's
favorite snack?

"Nice gnawing
you!"

Wood chips

Savanna Gathering

These animals are cooling off in the shade. Can you find all the hidden objects?

Art by Rich Powell

mitten

slice of pie

shoe

slice of pizza

comb

needle

bird

sailboat

bell

heart

ice-cream cone

fish

Going Bananas

There are 12 bananas hidden in this scene. Can you find them all?

Art by Iryna Bodnaruk

pencil

wedge of lemon

candy cane

banana

musical note

bowl

comb

candy corn

leaf

envelope

slice of pizza

toothbrush

ruler

pennant

tack

crescent moon

bell

It's a perfect day for an adventure! Can you find the hidden objects?

ladle

baseball bat

golf club

glove

traffic light

drinking straw

bowling pin

hanger   sailboat   fish   diamond   shoe   heart   piece of popcorn   baseball cap   boomerang

Art by Gary LaCoste

Sudsy Song

Can you find at least 11 differences between these two pictures?

Which sea creature haunts the ocean?

The boo whale

Where do whales go to get their braces fixed?

To the orca-dontist

Art by Tim Beaumont

What dip do bath towels eat at parties?

Shower cream and onion

Who stole the soap from the bathtub?

The robber ducky

Otter-ly Adorable Swimmers

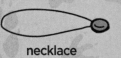

baseball bat

necklace

snowman

broccoli

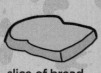

slice of bread

paper clip

baby bottle

crayon

mitten

See if you can find the hidden objects while these otters float and splash.

Art by Dana Regan

horseshoe

bow tie

nail

artist's brush

wishbone

ruler

ghost

fork

book

39

In-line Insects

Everyone's on the move today!
Can you find all the hidden objects?

bowl

sock

nail

butter knife

lightning bolt

lollipop

eyeglasses

mitten

crown

heart

book

spoon

toothbrush

Art by Pat Lewis

40

Savanna Speed

Can you find at least 21 differences between these two pictures?

THE SAVANNA BIKE RACE

THE SAVANNA BICYCLE RACE

Art by Paula Becker

Each of these small scenes contains **6** hidden objects from the list below. Some objects are hidden in more than one scene. Can you find the **6** hidden objects in each scene?

Hidden Object List

The numbers tell you how many times each object is hidden.

artist's brush (4)

button (2)

comb (4)

crescent moon (3)

drumstick (4)

envelope (2)

glove (4)

key (2)

needle (3)

paper airplane (3)

pencil (2)

sock (3)

BONUS
Two scenes contain the exact same set of hidden objects. Can you find that matching pair?

Art by Iryna Bodnaruk

43

Jungle Jubilation

Time to dress up and dance! Can you find the hidden objects?

crescent moon

cupcake

heart

star

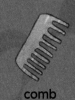
comb

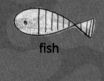
fish

sock

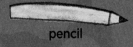
pencil

Art by Monika Filipina

Turtle Crossing

Can you help the baby turtles find a path down to the water? Be careful not to bump into birds blocking the way.

Art by Paula Becker

What is a turtle's favorite thing to wear?

A turtleneck

How does a turtle say goodbye?

"Turtle-oo!"

Water Balloon Toss

slice of
pizza

arrow

musical
note

hat

bell

lightning
bolt

crown

button

paper
airplane

heart

hot dog

iron

One, two, three, throw! See if you can find all the hidden objects.

fishhook

mitten

pickle

teacup

tack

lollipop

Art by Laura Close

bow tie

sailboat

paper clip

shoe

key

game piece

Tic Tac Row

What do the birds in each row (horizontally, vertically, and diagonally) have in common?

Art by Paul Richer

How did the fish cross the pond?

Very e-fish-iently

What is a fish's favorite country?

Finland

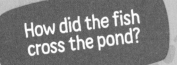

pencil

wedge of lemon

candy cane

banana

musical note

bowl

comb

candy corn

leaf

envelope

slice of pizza

toothbrush

ruler

pennant

tack

crescent moon

bell

you find all 21 chameleons hiding in this rain forest?

Tropical Painters

feather

hamburger

doughnut

ruler

slice of pizza

slice of lemon

cookie

cherries

carrot

flowerpot

ice-cream
cone

strawberry

slice of pie

banana

Art by Brian White

Hyenas love to laugh! See if you can find the hidden objects at the comedy show.

thimble

closed umbrella

belt

broccoli

lightning bolt

carrot

potato

puzzle piece

Art by Brian Michael Weaver

cleat

mitten

feather duster

glove

pencil

peanut

wristwatch

comb

banana

knitted hat

52

Just Sayin'

Give this bird something to say. Then find the hidden comb, ice-cream cone, pencil, plunger, and umbrella.

Art by James Kochalka

Each of these scenes contains 12 hidden objects, which are listed below. Find each object in one of the scenes, then cross it off the list.

Art by Kelly Kennedy

artist's brush	dog bone	needle	saltshaker
belt	fork	pants	skateboard
boomerang	ghost	pickax	spoon
candle	glove	piece of popcorn	sunglasses
cane	high-heeled shoe	ruler	wishbone
comb	lollipop	sailboat	yo-yo

Snowy Slide

ice-cream
cone

ladder

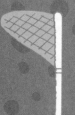

fishing net

sock

Art by Brian Michael Weaver

toothbrush

banana

hockey
stick

mitten

candy
cane

56

Can you hide this paw print in your own Hidden Pictures drawing?

Art by James Loram

Fishing with Friends

Can you find at least 15 differences between these two pictures?

What do you call a moose's facial hair?

A moose-stache

What's a raccoon's favorite snack?

Pop-coon

Why don't bears wear socks?

They have bear feet.

What do funny frogs sit on?

Silly pads

Art by Julissa Mora

Alpine Adventures

boot

ice-cream cone

carrot

banana

pie

balloon

pencil

star

car

crown

comb

spoon

The mountains are full of fun! Can you find all the hidden objects?

Art by Luke Flowers

ring

lollipop

bell

heart

slice of orange

key

umbrella

necktie

mug

slice of pizza

cellphone

toothbrush

feather

Slowly but Surely
These sloths are on the move!
See if you can find all the hidden objects.

pine tree

artist's brush

toothbrush

guitar

closed umbrella

musical note

teacup

mug

slice of pizza

cupcake

fork

scissors

lollipop

heart

ice-cream cone

envelope

flashlight

screwdriver

Art by Jennifer Harney

Flutter and Float

Can you find at least 17 differences between these two pictures?

Art by Brian Michael Weaver

Words and Objects

There are 8 words hidden in the left picture that match the 8 objects hidden below.
See if you can find them all.

Art by Brian White

What does an orangutan have before dinner?

An ape-etizer

Where do wild animals go to work out?

The jungle gym

Iguana Island

See if you can find the hidden objects while these iguanas sunbathe and splash.

ice cube

igloo

ice-cream cone

icicle

Art by Brian White

ice-cream cone

iron

ice skate

worm

Treetop Trails

Help Antonia find her way from START to FINISH along the branches.

Art by Andy Romanchik

Riverboat Tour

artist's brush

hockey stick

carrot

glove

canoe

fishhook

heart

magnet

ax

wedge of lemon

crown

crescent moon

waffle

balloon

jelly bean

There's a lot to see on the river! Can you find all the hidden objects?

Art by Gary LaCoste

pennant

drinking straw

needle

golf club

candle

scissors

ice-cream bar

comb

hanger

sock

toothbrush

piece of popcorn

bell

ladle

71

Parrot Pals

Each parrot has an exact match. Can you find all 10 pairs of parrots?

BONUS!
Find 15 hidden feathers.

Art by Maarten Lenoir

Which things in this picture are silly? It's up to you!

Art by Anna Jones

Swamp Singalong

pencil

drinking straw

flashlight

ladle

artist's brush

balloon

horseshoe

bell

boomerang

bowl

sock

heart

carrot

envelope

glove

ring

needle

crown

toothbrush

ruler

pennant

Art by Gary LaCoste

hanger   fishhook   banana   comb   slice of pie   piece of popcorn

Bird's Eye View

See if you can find all the hidden objects at the beach.

Art by Rich Powell

golf club

pencil

paper clip

shark

mitten

watermelon

fried egg

bowling ball

artist's brush

magnet

crown

hat

banana

heart

ring

flower

canoe

76

Firework Fascination

There are eight words (not pictures!) hidden in this scene. Can you find BLAST, BOOM, FUN, LOUD, POP, ROCKET, SKY, and SPARKLE?

Art by Susan Batori

Animal Toasts

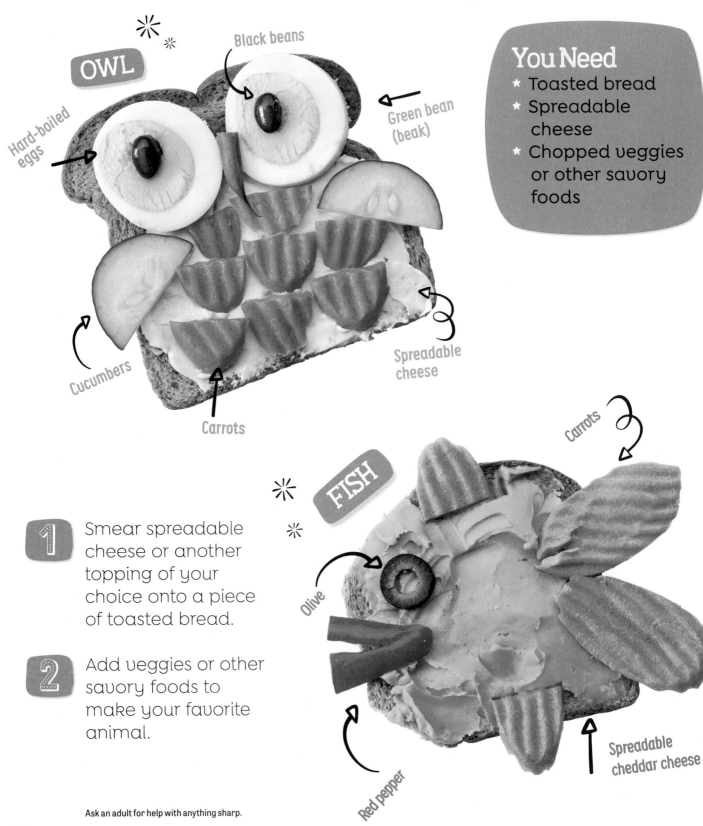

OWL

Black beans

Green bean (beak)

Hard-boiled eggs

Cucumbers

Carrots

Spreadable cheese

You Need
- ★ Toasted bread
- ★ Spreadable cheese
- ★ Chopped veggies or other savory foods

FISH

Olive

Red pepper

Carrots

Spreadable cheddar cheese

1 Smear spreadable cheese or another topping of your choice onto a piece of toasted bread.

2 Add veggies or other savory foods to make your favorite animal.

Ask an adult for help with anything sharp.

Shark Ball TOSS

A Game for 2 Players

You Need
* 2 two-liter plastic bottles
* Sandpaper or tape
* Acrylic paint
* Craft foam
* Tacky glue
* Tennis ball

To Play

Each player holds a "shark" by the cap end. Standing a few steps apart, players toss a tennis ball from shark to shark. How many times can you catch it in a row?

 For each "shark," cut the bottom 2 inches off a two-liter plastic bottle. Use sandpaper to smooth the edge, or cover it with tape.

 Paint the bottle with acrylic paint. Let it dry.

 Cut fins, eyes, and teeth from craft foam. Use tacky glue to attach them.

Ask an adult for help with anything sharp.

GLOW Bugs

Craft-Foam
Wings

Shampoo
Bottle

Scour-Pad
Wings

Glow-in-the-
Dark Puffy
Paint

Plastic
Egg

Beads Glued to
Fuzzy Sticks

1 Use a clean plastic bottle or egg for the body. Add eyes, legs, wings, and other decorations. (Try the ideas pictured.) Attach them using tacky craft glue or a low-temperature glue gun.

2 To make the bug glow, put a glow stick or a battery-powered tea light inside.

Ask an adult for help with anything sharp.

Missing-Mitten Puppet

You Need
* Yarn
* Mitten
* Wiggle eyes
* Felt
* Fabric glue
* Embroidery thread

Lost a mitten?
Use the one you have to make a puppet!

 Glue the yarn to the top of the mitten to make the mane. Let dry.

 Glue wiggle eyes to the front of the mitten.

3. Cut out a small felt triangle. Glue it on upside down to make the nose. For the mouth, cut a crescent shape from the felt. Glue it to the mitten just below the nose.

4. Cut four 3-inch strands of black embroidery thread. Glue them on the sides of the face to make the whiskers.

Ask an adult for help with anything sharp.

Planter Friend

You Need
* Plastic bottle
* Paper napkin
* Mod Podge
* Felt
* Glue
* Wiggle eyes
* Plant

 Cut a plastic bottle in half. Use the bottom half.

 Cut or tear the paper napkin into small pieces

 Cover the plastic bottle with Mod Podge. Stick the napkin pieces on the bottle. Cover with Mod Podge.

4 Cut shapes from felt to make ears, a nose, and a snout. Glue them to the bottle.

5 Add the wiggle eyes. Add the plant into the bottle. Give it water and sun.

Ask an adult for help with anything sharp.

82

Octo-Photo BUDDY

You Need
- ★ Thin cardboard
- ★ Poster board
- ★ Wiggle eyes
- ★ Paper clip
- ★ Tape
- ★ Photos
- ★ Ribbon

1 Cut an octopus head from thin cardboard. Cover it with poster board. Add wiggle eyes.

2 Cut eight arms and a hat from poster board. Glue them onto the head.

3 Draw on details.

4 Tape a paper clip to the back of each arm. Slide photos into the clips. Add a ribbon hanger.

Ask an adult for help with anything sharp.

LUMINOUS
Jellyfish

You Need

* Battery-powered string lights
* Umbrella
* Tape or low-temperature glue gun
* Pillow stuffing
* Sheer fabric
* Ribbons

What other animal costumes could you make using an umbrella?

 Attach battery-powered string lights to the top of an open umbrella using tape or a low-temperature glue gun. Attach the battery pack underneath.

 Glue or tape pillow stuffing evenly to the top of the umbrella, over the string lights.

 Cover the umbrella top with sheer fabric and tie the corners to the metal stretchers underneath.

Ask an adult for help with anything sharp.

 Glue or tape ribbons and battery-powered string lights to the umbrella's tips, letting them hang like jellyfish tentacles.

Bird Nest Spaghetti

You Need

* 4 ounces spaghetti, cooked and drained
* ½ cup shredded Parmesan cheese (half for sprinkling)
* ¼ cup shredded mozzarella cheese
* 2/3 cup marinara sauce
* Vegetable-oil spray
* ¼ cup cooked bacon bits or vegan-sausage crumbles

 1 Mix together the spaghetti, ¼ cup Parmesan cheese, mozzarella cheese, and marinara sauce in a large bowl.

 2 Grease a nonstick 6-cup muffin tin with vegetable-oil spray.

 3 Use tongs to evenly fill the muffin cups with the spaghetti mixture. Make a dent in the center of each cup to create the "nest."

 4 Sprinkle the bacon bits on top of the nests.

 5 Add the remaining Parmesan cheese over the nests.

 6 Bake at 375°F for 13–15 minutes or until set. Serve with extra sauce, if you wish.

Ask an adult for help with anything hot or sharp.

Critter Catchall

You Need
★ Yogurt cup
★ Acrylic paint
★ Felt
★ Tacky glue

 Paint an empty yogurt cup with acrylic paint. Let it dry.

 From felt, cut out an animal head, paws, and a tail.

 Use tacky glue to attach the shapes to the cup.

What fun objects could your new creation store?

Ask an adult for help with anything sharp.

Quilling Creatures

You Need
★ Paper
★ Skewer
★ Tacky glue
★ Toothpick
★ Wiggle eyes

 Cut paper into 11-inch-by-¼-inch strips.

 Roll a strip around a skewer. Slide it off, and let the circle loosen a bit.

 Use a toothpick to add a dab of tacky glue to secure the end of the paper. Let it dry.

 For a teardrop shape, pinch one end of the paper circle. For an oval, pinch both ends. For antennae, fold a strip in half and roll both ends.

 Add details such as wiggle eyes and paper stripes (as on the bee).

Bonus Ideas
To create a scene, glue the critters onto paper and draw around them. To make a greeting card, fold paper in half, glue a critter onto the front, and add a message. Ask an adult for help with anything sharp.

Feed the Elephant

You Need
- ★ Nut or coffee can
- ★ Felt
- ★ Glue
- ★ Thin cardboard
- ★ Wiggle eyes
- ★ Cardstock

 Cover a clean nut or coffee can with felt.

 Cut a head, a trunk, tusks, and ears from felt. Glue them together, then glue the head to thin cardboard. Add wiggle eyes. Glue the head to the can.

 For feet, glue four felt circles to the base. Add a felt tail.

4 Cut 20 peanuts from cardstock. Draw on lines.

5 Cut 28 cards from cardstock. Write P, E, A, N, U, and T on four cards each, one letter per card. Write Miss This Turn on two cards and Any Letter on the final two cards.

To Play

Give each player five peanuts. Shuffle the cards. Players take turns drawing cards until they can spell PEANUT. Once they do, they place a peanut into the can. Create a discard pile for used cards and reshuffle them to make another deck. The first player to feed all of their peanuts to the elephant wins.

Ask an adult for help with anything sharp.

Answers

▼ Pages 2–3

▼ Page 4

▼ Page 5

▼ Pages 6–7

▼ Page 8

▼ Pages 10–11

Answers

▼ Pages 12–13

▼ Pages 14–15

▼ Page 16

▼ Page 17

▼ Pages 18–19

▼ Page 20

Answers

▼ Page 21

▼ Pages 24–25

Worm **White on head** Same color	**Worm** **Yellow on neck**	**Worm** **Black on head** **Red breast**
Stripe on wing **White on head**	Stripe on wing **Yellow on neck** Same color **Red breast**	Stripe on wing **Black on head**
Beak **White on head** **Red breast**	**Beak** **Yellow on neck**	**Beak** **Black on head** Same color

▼ Pages 26–27

▼ Page 28

▼ Page 29

▼ Pages 30–31

Answers

▼ Page 32

▼ Page 33

▼ Pages 34–35

▼ Pages 36–37

▼ Pages 38–39

▼ Page 40

Answers

▼ Page 41

▼ Pages 42–43

▼ Page 44

▼ Page 45

▼ Pages 46–47

▼ Page 48

Answers

▼ Page 49

▼ Pages 50–51

▼ Page 52

▼ Page 53

▼ Pages 54–55

▼ Page 56

Answers

▼ Pages 60–61

▼ Pages 62–63

▼ Page 64

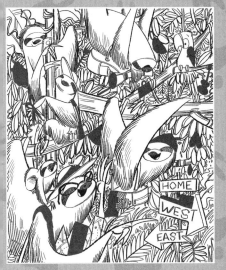

▼ Page 65

▼ Pages 66–67

▼ Page 68

▼ Page 69

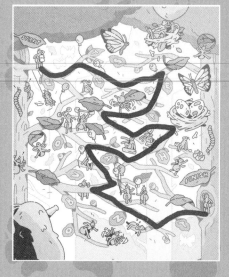

▼ Pages 70-71

▼ Page 72

▼ Pages 74-75

▼ Page 76

▼ Page 77

For information about permission to reprint
selections from this book, please contact
permissions@highlights.com.
Published by Highlights Press
815 Church Street
Honesdale, Pennsylvania 18431
ISBN: 978-1-63962-075-3
Manufactured in Shenzhen, Guangdong, China
Mfg. 06/2023
First edition
Visit our website at Highlights.com.
10 9 8 7 6 5 4 3 2 1
Cover art by Pat Lewis
Craft photos by Guy Cali Associates, Inc., except
animals (page 82)
iStock/Getty Images Plus/adogslifephoto, party hats
(page 82) iStock/Getty Images Plus/Nastco, banner,
confetti, balloon (page 82) iStock/Getty Images Plus/
leminuit

How does a camel hide?

What happened when the panda fell out of the tree?

What do you call a hippo that never stops eating?

What do you call an elephant with wings?

Why do tigers have stripes?

What do you call a penguin in the desert?

What game do sharks like to play?

What does a sloth read every morning?

How does a crocodile wake up its friends?

What did the platypus say when its meal arrived?

What do you call an eagle that can draw?

What do you call a dancing baboon?

2075C-01 © 2023 Highlights for Children, Inc.